supersensitive

spirited children
and teens

ONE
HEART

A resource for parents, carers and
teachers of highly sensitive children

Heather Carfrae Lyon

Supersensitive Spirited Children and Teens
Heather Lyon

First edition

Copyright © Heather Lyon, 2021.
Heather Lyon asserts her moral rights as the author of this work.

Cover image Wendy Miles

Cover design John Ravesi

Typesetting Michelle Pirovich thesqueezebox.com.au

ISBN 978-0-6452759-1-9
Also available as an ebook

DISCLAIMER

The material in this publication is of the nature of general comment only and does not represent professional advice. It is not intended to provide specific guidance for particular circumstances and it should not be relied on as the basis for any decision to take action or not take action on any matter which it covers. Readers should obtain professional advice where appropriate, before making any such decision. To the maximum extent permitted by law, the author and publisher disclaim all responsibility and liability to any person, arising directly or indirectly from any person taking or not taking action based on the information in this publication.

With love and gratitude to my family for their encouragement and inspiration

Acknowledgments

This book has its foundation in observations and knowledge gained from my studies and experience as a kindergarten teacher, parent and now grandparent.

Thank you to my teachers along the way, my lecturers, and the many families who have contributed to the stories and evidence of highly sensitive individuals in their families.

To the many children who enabled me to observe and hone my ideas and skills in working with their supersensitivity, you are the heroes of this book.

Highly sensitive and gifted staff in the teams I have led have taught me to question and not assume. There are many solutions to the myriad of challenges in a work day.

My life has been blessed with amazing friendships, and to those beautiful friends, a big thank you for the love and encouragement you have shown me while writing this book. The dinners, walks, long conversations, lunches and laughter has kept me going while following a road less travelled.

To Karen and Michelle, editor and designer, thank you – lets hope the journey continues. John thank you for the support, patience, and cover design. Wendy the beautiful image.

Barbara and Sophie for the courageous conversations and ongoing encouragement.

Family and close relationships are the foundation of all I do and I feel this book is just the beginning of a long and fruitful writing adventure.

For further information regarding training, and support programs visit www.supersensitivechildren.com or contact heather@supersensitivechildren.com

Contents

List of tables

About the author

Following an incredible career spanning over 40 years, Heather Carfrae Lyon has journeyed from being a kindergarten teacher to Chief Executive Officer to life coach, author and artist.

Highly sensitive, intuitive and psychic she was raised on a dairy farm in the rolling green hills of the Victorian countryside.

Heather has worked at a senior executive level in education, health, business, local government and a variety of organisations in the community sector. More recently she has written and facilitated programs and workshops supporting parents of supersensitive children and teens; it could be said that her career has come full circle.

Always an avid student, Heather has qualifications in early childhood development, education, management, leadership, life coaching and fine arts. She has been a member of several company boards including national not-for-profit organisations, a foundational school council, and a public hospital.

Her broad experience has given Heather a profound understanding of relationship dynamics and human behaviour, and she has nurtured and supported many other women seeking successful careers.

Now taking time to write and enjoy her artistic practice, she is excited to share her accumulated personal and professional wisdom.

Having observed her own two children and five grandchildren, it occurred to Heather that high sensitivity and intuition was a family trait and many other families she had been involved with had similar characteristics. These insights were the catalyst for this book.

Introduction

Living a spirited, intuitive, sensitive childhood has led me on the meandering path towards writing this book. When I was five, my lonely life was filled with fairies, imaginary friends and long days in nature. Now a grandmother, teacher, parent, artist, writer, CEO and student living alone once again, I can see the point of the amazing journey I have been on. My life has been the perfect lesson ... a springboard to helping the 20% plus of parents and children who are also highly intuitive, spirited and sensitive.

While everyone has a level of intuition and the capacity to be sensitive, the individuals I am describing here have these in bucket loads – a finely tuned and innate capacity; a gift or a curse depending upon your perspective.

Often gifted in a particular area, these individuals' characteristics can be described as a heightened ability in observation of both the environment, human behaviour, hearing, smell, taste, touch and often the unseen world. The ability to channel messages, see people who have passed over, see auras, feel energy, and tap into others' feelings often accompany these attributes.

Not all characteristics are present in every spirited, intuitive, highly sensitive person but many of the characteristics are, and it is their heightened way of reacting to and understanding of the world that puts them into this category.

This book has been a long time in the making but I have known about being highly sensitive all my life. Often called too sensitive, I would often sense how animals on our farm would behave, or when my parents were sad or upset, without being told. I had what some may call a sixth sense. Sometimes I could see an event before it happened. Deja vu was a common experience. A shadow for me, however, was not understanding that this was not everyone's experience.

It crystallised for me more fully when at kindergarten teachers' college I studied psychology learning about the varying influences on personality.

We had two amazing lecturers, Gerald Ashby and Doctor Ethel Hanby, who led us through the intricacies of individuation.

Led through the psyche of children I was mesmerised by stories of children who had differing gifts and amazing talents; some of these I knew from my volunteering at the Royal Children's Hospital. Observing babies and children as part of my teaching practice, once again I knew that some children exhibited more heightened intuition and sensitivity to their surroundings.

Later on, when I became a leader in organisations, I would know intuitively what was happening in the organisation before I had met the staff, or had briefings about them. While seemingly an advantage it did not bode well when I innocently questioned something which was a hidden secret in the organisation. One such secret involved horrific child abuse.

Later when working with children with terminal illness I was once again struck by the intuitive, sensitive and spirited personalities of many of these children. When my own children were born, I used my sensitivity to parent them. Being Sensitive, however, also meant that I second-guessed everything I did, even though it felt right. I also didn't follow the path set by the experts and sometimes found the offered advice was not appropriate for my children.

My two highly sensitive children discussed in more detail in this book taught me that many of the usual parenting strategies did not necessarily work for them. Sleeping, food allergies, high sensitivity to loud noises and an innate sixth sense were just a few.

Early in my career I studied for further qualifications in education, psychology, leadership and management and was introduced to the Myers–Briggs Type Indicator (MBTI) personality profiling. I began using the test in my work, and realised that many of the people scoring high in feeling and intuitive domains were in fact more highly sensitive to many aspects of human interaction and events. They were also more likely to be anxious in unfamiliar situations.

Based on the work of Carl Jung, the MBTI is one of the most widely used self-reporting personality tests for understanding psychological type and looks at how people operate in the world. The MBTI preferences indicate the differences in people that result from the following:

- where they prefer to focus their attention and get energy (extraversion or introversion)
- the way they prefer to take in information (sensing or intuition)
- the way they prefer to make decisions (thinking or feeling)
- how they orient themselves to the external world – with a judging process or a perceiving process (judging or perceiving).

Refined and developed further by Isabel Briggs Myers and Katherine Myers the test describes dynamic energy systems with interacting processes.[1]

There are varying opinions regarding the MBTI but using it for 20-plus years I have found that if it is administered in the correct conditions, the vast majority of people report that it accurately reflects their preferred way of operating in the world when they are relaxed.

The MBTI added to my repertoire of knowledge regarding the human condition and assisted my observational skills when working with both adults and children.

I have grandchildren and they are all highly sensitive in differing ways, and so I have embarked upon this journey in order to help them and many of the clients I see in my coaching practice; both adults and children.

After writing the first three chapters of this book I thought it would be sensible to see if anyone else was exploring the same subject. Oh, the wonderful power of the internet.

Elaine Aron, a psychologist from Portland Oregon, has spent her life studying highly sensitive people. Judith Orloff an American psychiatrist has written about her sensitivity and that of her clients and there is an institute of sensitivity in Holland. It was wonderful to find that my theories and observations had been studied and thoroughly investigated and there was much exciting news. However, I am keen to add my voice to the discussion and use my experience to teach other teachers and parents about sensitivity and spirited people from observations made in Australia and the United Kingdom while I was there studying mediumship and healing.

Okay, what does sensitive and spirited mean in this context? Aren't we all sensitive? Well, everyone exhibits some level of sensitivity; however, here we are talking highly sensitive – a 1 in 20 type of sensitivity – which is both a blessing and a curse.

What I am talking about is a heightened almost sixth sense about other people and their world. A heightened empathy, awareness to smells, sound, energetic fields of others, deep feelings and concern about the state of the world, extraordinary powers of observation and sometimes seeing peoples' energetic auras.

I use the term supersensitivity in this book to separate the usual definition of sensitivity from that of those with heightened sensitivity, sometimes referred to as overly sensitive, too sensitive, or other terms such as prickly or lacking resilience when responding to certain stimuli. In many contexts, heightened sensitivity is seen as a problem rather than part of the continuum of normal human responses.

Many of these children are gifted in some way and have exceptional physical skills. Years of teaching and observations of young children have led me to the conclusion that these children make up at least 20% of the population and often have difficulty fitting into the current education system.

Elaine Aron concurs in *The Highly Sensitive Child*, stating a common inherited trait is high sensitivity, found in about 15 to 20% of children (the percentage is the same in boys and girls).[2]

The other dimension of supersensitivity is that of psychic ability. My observations over 40 years of working with children, their families and in organisations at all levels have led me to conclude that while many Sensitives are psychic, not all psychics are what is termed Sensitive. A much higher portion of supersensitives have extremely high intuition and many of the Sensitive children I have known and worked with have spoken about angels, fairies, gnomes, energy people and light people.

This is the area which intrigues me the most as I had amazing experiences overseas which I will discuss further in Chapter 7 and which will not be for everyone and nor do I profess to be an expert on psychic intuition but merely sharing my experiences and that of other parents and children. Psychic intuition in this context is referring to the ability of sometimes sensing an event that may happen in the future and also seeing or feeling situations from the past and accurately describing them.

Chapter 1

Identifying a supersensitive spirited child

Our family story

Your baby is a highly sensitive baby and your family thinks it is a problem with the way you are parenting this very special person. You have read all the parenting books and no matter what you do she just won't sleep easily; in fact, she stays awake much longer than other babies.

She is very alert and watches you as you move around the room. She startles easily and cries when the car starts. Strangers bother her from a young age and it is impossible to give her a bottle; she gags at a bottle and a dummy and so you keep breastfeeding her until she is about 13 months when she announces, "Brekky, Daddy".

She talks and walks early (even though she was born six weeks prematurely), will only wear certain clothes and wants to wear them day after day even when they are dirty... a dinosaur outfit is worn every day for about three weeks. She doesn't like textured or scratchy clothes. She talks about fairies and has imaginary friends. Her favourite story at age two is *Jethro Byrd, Fairy Child*. A book usually considered more suitable for seven- or eight-year-olds.

She is incredibly insightful. Aged about two and a half, the museum is one of her favourite places and she asks to go to the one in her new suburb. She is very surprised that there is only one in Melbourne because how will kids learn that information?

At two she compliments adults on their appearance noticing different shoes and best clothes. She introduces herself using her full name and enquires of adults about their surnames and middle names. She will listen to several stories in a row and likes complicated plots in storybooks. She announces that she needs an instruction book to use on a climbing frame and then uses the book to organise older children into a game. She argues with her parents and has compelling reasons for not doing something.

At four she has bad nightmares and takes herself out of children's movies which are too scary. She is worried when teachers don't do what they say they will; and children miss out on turns because it is unfair. She has an amazing memory and a quirky way of problem solving.

Not long after her baby sister is born, she tells her mother, "I wish we could go back to the olden days".

Her mother asks, "Oh, when Gran or Mummy were young?"

"No," she replies, "before my sister was born"!

She scores 22 on Aron's Sensitive Child Checklist.[3]

The first few school years are miserable and she does not want to get out of bed because boys are being mean to her and the teacher doesn't understand her. She becomes extremely depressed and her parents take her to a psychologist who specialises in gifted children. He indicates that she is gifted in some areas and behind in some. Her parents go to see the school principal to discuss her problems and are told most parents think their child is gifted, she just needs to be resilient and fit in.

Her parents find a school which accepts and understands her supersensitivity and spirited nature and she has a teacher who gets her. She now mostly enjoys school with this new understanding.

This story, or elements of it, is a common one for spirited and sensitive children.

***

So, what does being a supersensitive spirited child look like? (please note, I will also further refer to supersensitive spirited child/children as Sensitive/s, Sensitive child/children.)

As previously mentioned, at least 15 to 20% of the population would be characterised as highly sensitive and spirited.[4] The areas I have used to categorise supersensitivity are those which I have used when planning and evaluating activities to further enhance children's development in early childhood settings as a teacher, and in my coaching.

These categories include social, emotional, spiritual/intuitive, intellectual and physical. I would like to reiterate here that not all Sensitives exhibit all characteristics in every domain. I have added a spiritual/intuitive dimension which may be a new concept for many parents and teachers; however, from my work with teachers and parents, personal experience and observations within my family this is an area which is not often acknowledged or discussed.

Checklist for a Sensitive

When scoring on this checklist, as an indicator most Sensitives would score at least 15 plus.

Sometimes, however, a child will tick all the boxes in one or two domains and not many in the others; it just means they are more sensitive to specific stimuli.

Table 1. Checklist for a supersensitive spirited child

Social development

☐ As a baby often demonstrates early milestones.

☐ Smiles and talks early.

☐ Has sophisticated ways of communicating compared with peers of the same age.

☐ Can engage in complicated games with older children and understands the rules.

☐ Makes up their own complex games and sometimes becomes frustrated with peers who don't want to engage in their games.

☐ A leader in groups and has highly creative play ideas.

☐ Very aware of differences and unfairness, and will advocate for others.

- [ ] Likes complicated discussions and understands sophisticated concepts appropriate for much older children.
- [ ] Likes to cooperate with adults and older children unless feels disrespected by them.
- [ ] Is very aware of strangers at an early age and will avoid interacting with them.
- [ ] Takes time to warm up to new situations and sometimes chooses not to interact with new people until they have had time to make their own assessments.

Intellectual development

- [ ] Sophisticated conversations and complex ideas at a very young age.
- [ ] Often has a deep understanding of particular topics which engage them.
- [ ] Finds innovative ways to solve problems.
- [ ] Aware of social norms and rules and will remind adults and peers of them.
- [ ] Uses complex language patterns.
- [ ] Has an extremely well-developed vocabulary.
- [ ] Plans and understands past, present and future.
- [ ] Can concentrate for long periods and objects to interruptions.

Physical development

- [ ] Often challenges themself and will practise a skill until highly competent.
- [ ] Often skilfully walks, runs and climbs early.
- [ ] Sometimes is the quiet observer, practising a skill when no adults are watching until they can do the task completely.
- [ ] Likes team sports but gets stressed if put under pressure or feels they are letting the team down.
- [ ] Often very competent at a number of sports.

☐ Often complains of itchy or scratchy clothing.

Emotional development

☐ Highly sensitive to praise and criticism.

☐ Can read social situations and will withdraw if other children are being loud or aggressive.

☐ If an extroverted Sensitive, may join in games and become over-stimulated and then find it difficult to wind down.

☐ May become upset and querulous if adults don't follow through with agreed-upon plans.

☐ Able to express their own feelings and interpret others accurately.

☐ Prone to over-stimulation in stressful situations.

☐ May become withdrawn or feel sick when they have to perform in front of an audience.

☐ Worries and fears or vivid dreams often interrupt their sleep.

☐ Worries and thinks deeply about worldly issues.

☐ Highly attuned to others' feelings and can become the advocate for others.

☐ Can see unfairness in situations and will call it out.

☐ Don't want to sleep in their own bed because they have seen scary people.

☐ Very particular about what they wear.

☐ Very sensitive and compassionate to animals and their needs.

Spiritual/intuitive development

☐ Sees or talks about angels in conversation.

☐ Talks about energy, feeling energy or sees sparkles of energy or auras (human energy fields).

☐ Is particularly in tune with others' hurt or sad feelings.

☐ Talks about or sees people who have died.

- [ ] May not want to go into some places or rooms because it is scary and doesn't feel right.
- [ ] Will sometimes initiate sophisticated discussions about heaven, God or people who have died.
- [ ] Has premonitions; for example, will describe situations they have seen happening on the other side of the world which they cannot have possibly known about (deja vu), such as a train crash in another country.
- [ ] Incredibly observant about changes and differences in their surroundings.

Chapter 2

Parenting Sensitives

Change is part of life; however, life is now advancing at a dizzying pace.

I remember my father telling me about the day when Amelia Earhart landed on the beach in her tiny plane in the 1930s as part of her attempt to circumnavigate the world. It was to take her six months, a trip which would now take about 48 hours. A television and refrigerator were new and exciting additions to our house during my primary school years as was the first Holden car.

Fast-forward to today and we now watch news as it happens around the world but often don't know the names of our neighbours. Refrigerators now have computers to order the groceries and dispense ice. Cars now can park without the driver's input. Life is very different and often people don't have the skills or energy to connect to each other.

One of the few preschool children's TV programs back then was *Play School*. Now, almost all school children have a laptop or tablet and a mobile phone in their school bags. Where toddlers once played with books, blocks or pull-along toys at the doctor's surgery, they now sit viewing movies or games on an iPad or their mum's phone. So how do parents now tap into their innate wisdom in guiding their children, particularly Sensitive children, through numerous and rapid changes?

As a new parent in the 1970s, my advice came from parents, my teacher training, friends and reference books. This allowed me to make my own parenting decisions through observing and engaging with our children using much intuition and good old "trial and error".

Parenting advice

Now parenting advice is everywhere: television, Dr Google, Facebook, Twitter, and in numerous parenting books. It takes an incredibly resilient parent to ignore the plethora of parenting advice and parent their children according to their own values and instincts, particularly if their child is spirited and sensitive. I know parents who often doubt their own wisdom and turn to technology and others for ratification of their decisions, fearing they were too harsh or unfair.

> *Parenting is a personal choice and I have found that*
> *children want to be parented with respect; the most*
> *important concern for them is to be trusted and listened to.*

How do parents have the self-assurance to follow their intuition and inner knowing, particularly when their child is one of the 15 to 20% who are spirited and highly sensitive? The answers in the example below go some way to answering this question.

Parenting groups questionnaires

In feedback from workshops I conducted with children aged from four to 13, I asked them two questions. The first question being: What do you want most from your parents? The response in its many forms was essentially for parents "to spend time playing with me" and to "really listen to me when I am talking". These requests seem simple enough but many of the comments were followed by explanations involving Mummy constantly looking at her phone, and Daddy looking at his phone or sending emails.

Children in workshops, particularly those aged eight and above wanted their parents to let them trust their own judgement in areas such as food choices and bedtimes.

One enterprising and frustrated supersensitive seven-year-old wrote her father a letter regarding parents really listening to children. The family were looking for a new house and spent weekends at open for inspections, making offers which were not accepted, and searching for properties to buy most evenings. It was a particularly stressful time for them too as the overheated property market meant prices increasing by $50,000 to $100,000 in a matter of months.

Her letter read: *Dear Alex, I don't like you because you just look at your phone and houses all the time and don't play with Gus and I or talk to us. I want you to stop.*

A dilemma as the new house was for everyone. The parents gave up house hunting for a few months and discretely viewed houses when the children were not around.

The second question I asked was: What do you think your parents want for you? The essence of the answers was to be "happy and healthy children". What common sense and wisdom from four-year-olds.

What do children want most from their parents?

Gitta, aged eight: "Time to play with me, and to really listen to me when I am talking. Not be looking at their phone and going, 'Ah ha, ah ha, that's good'."

My approach

My parenting was more open-ended and mostly permissive with the occasional strict interlude. My children now call it parenting by guilt! So how did this work? Our family shared meals together and talked about our day and the children's activities.

When they started going to parties and sleepovers as teenagers we would talk about drugs and alcohol, and also travelling in cars with peers who had been drinking. We would say, "You can go, but it's your responsibility". That was our mantra be it regarding their homework, parties or events where there might be decisions they needed to make about alcohol and drugs or dangerous activities.

These were the days where there were no mobile phones and nightclubs were the go-to places. The term helicopter parenting was not a commonly used term, and it was far more common for parents to be less involved in every activity teens undertook. Strict parents controlled where children went but could not check in to their play activities to the same degree we can today with technology. We did have a policy of picking them up from wherever; even if it was 3 am it gave us some comfort to know they got home safely.

Because both of our children were supersensitives, the decisions they made included using their intuition. Change and transitions were part of the norm for them and in hindsight, we parented well in some areas but in others we probably left a lot to chance... not a good tactic for introverted supersensitives.

We moved house about every five years or less as our supersensitive son pointed out when we had been in a house for almost six years. "Mum," he would comment, "we have been here more than five years. When will we be moving?" We had no intention of moving; however, he was obviously more tuned in than we were because we found a house closer to the beach and moved there three months later.

Children now travel much more and generally spend more time having adventures with their families, which involves overseas holidays, new schools if the current one doesn't work out or activities after school. Apart from technological change they are exposed to changes in the world daily through the many forms of technology. It is therefore extremely difficult to protect them from disturbing and age-inappropriate information.

From my early childhood studies I am aware that images of war and violence are particularly damaging to young children who are unable developmentally to determine and process fact from fiction until about age seven.

While they may articulate, "It's only pretend", evidence suggests the actual processing leading to true comprehension is formed along with moral judgement at around eight years of age.

Supersensitive children, due to their heightened feelings, will often have ongoing nightmares and act out situations which have frightened them and they are unable to understand. I have observed some gender differences here, with boys often imitating what they have viewed with violent play. Parents not understanding this is part of their child's developmental response, react with admonishing words or punishment. Girls, however, are more likely to have fearful dreams and play out the activities with dolls or toy animals.

What science tells us

There has been much research done on temperament, anxiety and personality relating to sensitivity, as well as recent research into the impact of certain genes that delves even further and considers the challenges faced by people dealing with these inherited traits.

Having worked with the Myer–Briggs Type Indicator (MBTI), I have come to the conclusion that supersensitive children are born with these traits and this influences how they interact with their environment.

The MBTI personality test is based on the work of Carl Jung and developed by mother and daughter Katherine Cook Briggs and Isabel Briggs Myers and is a non-judgemental self-assessment tool that views the strengths and gifts of individuals. Divided into 16 types, the test looks at psychological type which defines the characteristics in which individuals gather information and orient themselves in the world.

I have used and studied the MBTI since 1986 and being involved with over 500 individual tests, I am convinced that personality or temperament determines supersensitivity, particularly empathic behaviour, and individuals exhibiting the feeling and intuition functions are more likely to have a high correlation with Sensitive traits.

The more recent gene research appears to support this. In her book Gene Genius Dr Margaret Smith discusses what she calls the warrior and worrier genes and their impact on our stress reaction. Different genes determine the bodies reaction to heightened stimuli, and the production of certain enzymes as a physical response. Individual reactions are influenced by their inherited gene pool.[5]

Families often speak about children being like one of their ancestors who is remembered for their unique sensitivity. In four generations of my family, I can identify a parent or grandparent who was a Sensitive. For further information refer to *Gene Genius* by Dr Margaret Smith with Sue Williams.[6]

As a student at art school, I am amazed at the number of Sensitive individuals enrolled in this creative study. Does this mean that genes determine creativity or are other factors such as environment at play here? I would argue that supersensitivity is most likely to be genetically determined.

Change

Knowing your child is hard wired to being anxious will perhaps be reassuring to parents whose first reaction to resistance to change is to blame their own parenting. Change is very stressful for many Sensitives, and children need support, education and encouragement to manage their anxiety.

> *Let's also remember, on the flip side, that Sensitives are often very good at supporting others through new situations, and can thrive and lead when given the appropriate encouragement and support to follow their own intuition.*

As a leader in organisations, it was very easy for me to adapt to change if I was able to plan the implementation and explore the impact on people before following through with the government's or Board's decisions. Blessed with what I would call almost a second sense, I would often be able to read what was coming and prepare strategies for staff and clients to understand the decisions… even if we didn't agree with them.

If you are a Sensitive then you will be often able to use these skills of knowingness to parent your child through the changes. If you are not, then careful planning and following your child's lead in answering their concerns will make managing change less stressful for everyone. Your confidence that everything will be okay will also reassure them. Be aware that supersensitives are very attuned to non-verbal indicators, sensing when you are not being truthful, they will be the first to notice and highlight this.

What about a parent who is not a supersensitive who is parenting a child who is? Aron suggests that a Sensitive child knows your weaknesses all too well.[7] They may also call you out on inconsistencies particularly if you have been untruthful or asked them not to divulge something they disagree with. My three-year-old son commented about my decision about having one of his sister's friends over to play: "Heather, is that a good idea?" He had remembered I had given an early to bed instruction as his sister had been teary and overtired the day before.

My supersensitive granddaughter commonly had discussions with teachers about their teaching methods, particularly if they were not explaining the subject in a way which could be understood by all students. Teachers often found this challenging; however, when they understood that it was coming from a place of advocacy rather than impertinence, they modified their teaching methods to be more inclusive.

From personal experience as an extroverted supersensitive I often found myself in advocacy roles for my peers who were not confident to highlight unfair or inconsistent behaviour with a non-supersensitive teacher.

While it may be frustrating at times waiting for your supersensitive child to adapt to stressful or new situations, your patience will be rewarded when they appreciate your support. Their powers of observation may sometimes help you avoid dangerous or embarrassing situations. Your support will also help them to develop resilience and negotiating skills when dealing with other non-supersensitives.

Chapter 3

Sensitive babies and toddlers

My passion about and understanding of babies and toddlers began when I taught and coordinated toddler groups. These toddler groups were run through local councils and were funded by the Victorian Government. Operating in Maternal and Child Health Centres, parents attended with their children aged from birth to three years.

With early childhood teacher training and postgraduate studies focused on the first eight years of life, I had a special interest in the developmental age when babies begin to engage with the world through to when they attend four-year-old kindergarten.

My other role at that time was running the child study program at The Institute of Early Childhood Development. I worked with students observing mothers' and toddlers' play and parenting styles through an observation booth.

My daughter Rachel was one of the children participating in the study and it was her behaviour and subsequent discussions with the students in tutorials that caused me to realise her behaviour was quite different to that of the other six toddlers.

She was relaxed in exploring her environment and while the other children hovered near their mothers, she explored the room in a confident carefree manner. At the time I just explained it away as being very familiar with her surroundings as she attended other groups I organised and I was sure some of the confidence came from that.

The same cannot be said for our son Alex who would happily explore, but the minute I interacted with another child he would run back to me and glare at the other child and state: "That's my mum." Needless to say, he only came with me a couple of times!

I had studied attachment behaviour but I was sure there was more to it. It was the same when I was teaching kindergarten groups. I always referred back to my child development books but they did not explain the extremes of behaviour and relating at either end of the spectrum. I had also worked with children with autism and ADHD (attention deficit hyperactivity disorder) diagnoses, but this was different.

Traits

These children as babies and toddlers had almost a sixth sense and could negotiate with adults in a sophisticated way. They usually had knowledge about a particular subject way beyond their years and they had other quirky traits as well.

Some were particularly skilled at puzzles, would have amazing bonds with animals or could use their physical prowess to climb trees, ride bikes or competently undertake other physical activities which their much older peers were confronted by. These were the supersensitive spirited children who we now know make up at least 15 to 20% of the population.

Two of my grandchildren have these amazing skills and dedication to their sport. One is able to water ski at a level that defeats most adults. The other is an extremely dedicated and talented gymnast. The skills they possess isn't the only remarkable part, it is also the dedication and willingness to practise until they attain the level they are happy with.

Supersensitive Spirited Children and Teens

Chapter 4

Sensitives and sleep

When I was a CEO of a mother and baby's hospital and on the Board of a parenting research organisation, you could be reassured that I knew a lot about babies and sleeping. I managed a dedicated team of nurses with extensive expertise on the subject. I also chaired a research project about babies' sleeping habits.

Referrals for the sleeping program came from a variety of sources and there was a waiting list to attend the programs. After a three or four-day stay, most sleeping issues were sorted and families departed smiling and confident. There were, however, some babies who continued to concern the staff and this led me to question why.

My intuition, sensitivity and personal experience told me that there was more to it. Was there something else at play in the science and the methods of supporting babies to sleep easily?

Sleep school

A fairly typical day at sleep school would involve parents arriving for either a long-term stay or a day stay. They would be welcomed by the highly trained and experienced staff, settled into a room, and then a dedicated staff member would talk them through the process of observing their baby to get to know their sleepy signals, particular cries and routines.

There is something about a crying baby that brings out my greatest mothering and rescuing feelings. Something I cannot rationally explain as to why. Intellectually, I can rationalise the philosophy of letting a baby cry for short periods when they are tired, but emotionally, my heart goes into meltdown and my first reaction is to run in and pick up the baby and immediately sooth it.

One particular day, it took all my strength not to do this.

My vivid memory is chairing a meeting in a room near the day stay program, where the crying of the child in the next room was so painful for me, I could hardly concentrate. I kept thinking, please pick him up, go in now. I somehow knew it was a little boy. It felt like hours before someone responded, but in reality, it was probably only about two minutes. In this time, I knew intuitively there were other factors at play. Was it the child's supersensitive temperament which was contributing to this?

I left this position and for years after had a niggling feeling – my intuition was telling me to look further into this issue.

Further observations

This was cemented further when my first grandchild was born. She was born six weeks early and spent the first two weeks of her life in hospital. Her sleeping patterns were obviously interrupted by this, but even with all the suggested sleep support methods, as she grew older, she remained awake. She did not fit any patterns. Her parents tried desperately to get her to sleep but a quietly sleeping baby refused to materialise.

As life continued and she tested her parents further, I began to reflect on family patterns and remembered that my own children, our daughter and son, had had different and uneven sleep patterns. I also remembered my mother telling me I was a nightmare to get to sleep. Was this inexperienced parenting or was there something else at play?

The penny finally dropped when I was managing a group of skilled maternal and child health nurses. They were highly trained and experienced women with families and rich life experiences. One day in a meeting, when debriefing after an eventful week, one of them talked about a highly sensitive baby with a father to match, and suddenly it made sense. Methods which worked for most babies did not work for about one or two in 20 babies.

These nurses knew that they needed to fully resource these parents to cope with these supersensitive babies, including assuring them their baby was normal, and encouraging them to follow their intuition when parenting.

If you have a Sensitive baby who doesn't behave as most other children do, take heart because you have been given a gift and you will eventually get some sleep!

Alexander our son was the perfect breastfed baby, sleeping eating, eating sleeping, until he was introduced to solid food and that's when the nightmare began.

The calm perfect baby suddenly began crying (actually screaming) at about four o'clock in the afternoon almost every day; he also began to not sleep well at night. I took him to the doctor and to the Maternal Child and Health Centre, but they could find nothing wrong with him.

I knew something wasn't right and as I was a kindergarten teacher, I knew about child development and as this was my second child, I thought I could figure it out. I listened to all the advice and tried everything: breastfeeding him again, putting him on his tummy with a hot water bottle, cuddling him, letting him cry, playing music, taking him for long drives in the car.

I was so tired and exhausted just functioning every day. Working part time, studying, looking after my three-year-old daughter and surviving while my husband worked long hours and was overseas for the occasional long stint.

Alexander began losing weight over the next few months and the maternal and child health nurse suggested visiting a paediatrician as he also had asthma and was often taking antibiotics for chest infections. My first visit was both an amazing relief and a trial. Following a battery of tests, including copious blood tests, the diagnosis was that he lacked the enzymes to break down sucrose. He was given a highly restrictive diet. This diet included no sugar, measuring almost everything including amounts of fruit and vegetables – down to the last teaspoon, and reading every packet of breakfast cereal or processed food for ingredient listings.

Alexander's sleep patterns at that time were weird and wonderful at the same time. He would often come into our bed for a conversation in the middle of the night when he couldn't sleep. He would hop into our bed and settle after the reassuring conversation about: "Had it rained in Africa and would the children there have water to drink now?" Other times he would wake us up announcing, "I have finished playing Lego and had my milk and snack of apple and cheese, and now I'm going to sleep". It could be 11 pm and we had been asleep for a couple of hours!

Another of Alexander's night adventures occurred when his father, in desperation, took the handle off the inside of his bedroom door as he wouldn't stay in his room (not something I would recommend, ever), only to have him knock at the front door and announce, "I couldn't open the door so I came this way". He had climbed out his bedroom window. He was two and a half years old and it was 10 pm! In hindsight, the decision to accept that I was not Super Mum and ask for more support from family and friends, enabled me to survive those long nights with Alexander and his unpredictable sleeping habits.

Looking back at the things we tried, makes me want to both laugh and cry. I realise that Alexander is a supersensitive and he exhibited many of the characteristics common in these children. He is amazingly perceptive about people, has an incredible memory, is very tuned into what is happening around him, has an intuitive sense about the future and is warm and funny.

As a child he hated clothes that were not matching or scratchy, and certain bedclothes either because of the non-matching colours or the feel. One day I recall helping him with his clothes for kindergarten. He had blue-and-red boots, a blue skivvy, red jumper and blue jeans and red socks. His green undies did not fit the colour scheme and I remember reassuring him no one would see them so it wouldn't matter. He looked at me and in floods of tears and commented: "But *I* know!"

> *My granddaughter has the same issues with the texture and colour of clothes, and her sleeping patterns are also similar. Alexander's son doesn't like seams in socks as they irritate him. His cousin doesn't like scratchy underpants and won't wear socks. His mum hated wearing anything made from wool next to her skin. It's a family thing, this highly sensitive behaviour. Issues such as these are common for Sensitive children.*

I found it easier to plan for stressful situations, anticipating what might concern Alexander and therefore avoid the meltdown. His meltdowns shifted very quickly and he managed his diet extremely well, negotiating the sugar-laden food at birthdays and politely refusing lollies offered by well-meaning family and friends. Things only became a challenge when other parents didn't understand his diet and encouraged him to eat foods, they thought were good for him. He would then suffer from a swollen, sore stomach and diarrhea.

Our daughter Rachel's sensitivity manifested in other ways. Extremely sensitive to light she slept with a bassinet liner over her head. If this was removed, she would wake up and scream. Her sleeping patterns were also disturbed particularly by noises. The first 18 months of her life were spent in a terrace house in the city. Truck and bus sirens and noisy cars were part of the everyday landscape, so keeping the house quiet was difficult with this Sensitive sleeper. With the bassinet liner over her head much like a tent, she held onto the edge of this muslin material and sucked her thumb; this seemed to sooth her and her sleeping patterns improved.

A change of scene, such as travelling in the car, or moving from the bassinet into a cot, or cot to bed, would be enough to have her awake and irritable for nights on end. The bassinet liner went with her as her security blanket and this coupled with thumb sucking continued until well after she started school. Luckily, I was confident enough to fend off criticism from well-meaning friends and family, and to continue to support these methods of soothing. Sensitive children will often have rituals and support systems to relieve their anxieties in stressful situations.

Alexander's support system for bed included a satin-edged blanket, a bottle and a dummy. He was breastfed until he was 18 months old but went to family day care when he was about 15 months old and added a bottle to his repertoire of sleep support items. He maintained all of these until he went to school (despite the disapproving looks and comments) as his security system and night-time soothers. He has grown up to be a confident, happy adult. I am sure the childhood security system helped! It certainly helped with settling him and helping him to sleep.

Genetic trait or family patterning?

Achieving a good night's sleep is something which has been difficult for me for most of my life.

Highly sensitive to noise inside or outside the house, a possum on the roof or the squeak of the gate, the wind in the trees, any form of light in the room, my partner's breathing, are all things which are enough to keep me awake, stressing about how many hours I have left to sleep. Anxiety about locked doors and windows, and early morning appointments such as being on time for my personal training, are enough to keep me awake mulling over the past or future for hours. Herbal sleeping preparations mostly help but then

I stress about the effects of these too!

> *Supersensitivity in our family manifests in children who either are extremely difficult to settle at bedtime and who perhaps need less sleep or get less sleep because of their sensitivity.*

Discovering this was the final piece of the puzzle and answered the questioning which had begun on that first day at the mother's and baby's hospital.

Tips for parents and caregivers

These are some tactics I found useful in my roles as a parent, teacher and grandparent in settling and reassuring Sensitive babies and small children at rest time or sleep time. My philosophy regarding sleeping has relaxed over the years but I have found spending five to 10 minutes of reassuring time can prevent constant calling out and tears.

Table 2. Settling tips for Sensitives

- Make sure the noise level and surrounding environment is as quiet and calm as possible. Sometimes calming music can help as can familiar routines and security items, such as a special blanket or teddy.
- Routines such as bath, warm milk, then teeth and stories.
- Often a reassuring lie beside and patting or back scratching can help calm your Sensitive restless child. I often found my presence was enough; other times forehead rubs or a back rub would do the trick.
- Between about 18 months and five years of age, many children like the comfort of sleeping in their parents' bed. This need often coincides with scary dreams and can be influenced by the sorts of programs children watch on TV. Sensitive children are often particularly imaginative and the fluffy monster you and their non-Sensitive peers see as harmless, may be terrifying to them in the darkness.

- Take their fears seriously and remember that because you can't see something in their room doesn't mean that it is not real for them.

- Keep their sleeping area uncluttered except for those soft toys and security items and offer a night light.

- If sharing a room, have the Sensitive child go to bed and settle first.

- Give them time to wind down from the day, and this means quiet activities not television or screen time, at least an hour before going to bed.

- Be confident you know your child best and choose whatever works best for you both. Some parents start with the child in bed with them and then move them later. Another family I know bought a king-sized bed with room for everyone.

- Sometimes a bath or shower will assist with washing away the stress of the day.

- All children go through stages and nothing lasts forever so enjoy them at every age; your Sensitive child will give you amazing joy and satisfaction when you take time to understand their needs.

Chapter 5

Sensitives at childcare, kindergarten and school

When your Sensitive child starts childcare and/or kindergarten, it is an enormous change – much the same as starting a new job or many other transitions we are familiar with such as a new relationship, a new sibling, a change in living circumstances and moving to another state or country. Remember when you did any or all of these things how you felt... excited, anxious, worried, sick, energised, tentative, fearful. A Sensitive child myself, these were all things which I can remember experiencing.

It is the same for these children but greatly magnified as their energy system is tuned to take in the experience but not yet finely tuned enough to adapt to unknown circumstances. How you manage this will be critical to their success.

Make sure you are in a good space to support them about where they will be going and anticipate possible glitches. Have written information about your child readily available. This will support the teachers or carers to ensure a smooth transition.

Don't assume what has worked for others will necessarily work for your child. Use your knowledge and intuition to guide you. Remember, you are the expert advocate for your child, listen to other opinions but keep your own counsel.

Be confident to request special treatment such as wearing earphones in a loud and busy room. Many Sensitives are overwhelmed by lots of noise.

Make the teacher aware and point them to resources such as Aron's The Highly Sensitive Child. At least 15 to 20% of children are Sensitives, so the chance of there being at least one in the classroom is extremely high.

Choosing childcare

This will be a major milestone for you both. Choosing the right childcare is hard for any parent. If your child is highly sensitive and you are not, being aware of the stressors for your child are extremely important here.

Your child will need you to be their advocate and not be overcome by the stress of finding an appropriate education and care facility, by taking the first available vacancy. Make sure you have visited the centre and evaluated the quality of care because leaving your Sensitive child in circumstances where they do not feel safe and secure could have serious long-term repercussions for them trusting people, also for their mental health.

I recently had to support a colleague who was making a child protection notification following a visit to a so-called reputable childcare centre. She was so traumatised she needed counselling following the visit. Why mention this? One of the policies was the centre did not allow parents into the childcare rooms. Parents had accepted this as normal practice. She spoke to professional, competent parents who had accepted this policy. The quality of the care and the skills of the staff did not comply to the basic regulations, although the marketing was very slick and sophisticated.

So how to avoid this type of situation and find childcare which suits Sensitive children? Local government has staff who can give you information about how to find childcare available in your local area. Go to your local childcare centre and ask to observe the program and room your child will be placed in. Ask other parents about their experiences. Maternal and child health staff can give you reading matter to help you decide. Ratings of programs in relation to legislated standards are available online and will give you a starting point.

If you are supersensitive then you will have tuned into what is happening at the centre using your intuition. Feel confident you will know the right questions to ask. Ensure you have time to talk and observe the program. Look at how children are greeted, at how staff interact with each other: Are staff conversing over the children or making sure they are on a level where eye contact and facial expressions are tuned into? Observe how welcome you feel as you need to feel reassured that your child will be comfortable asking for help when you are not there.

Act confidently when discussing you child's sensitivity. If the reaction is not one of empathetic support then you may need to look elsewhere.

Younger children cannot tell you what has happened during the day. One bad experience might mean that they will not trust you for other new experiences.

Supersensitive children are highly influenced by non-verbal interactions, so watch their reactions to staff.
A supersensitive child who cries and regularly pulls away from a carer or particular relative may be giving you non-verbal signals that they do not feel safe with this person. This is a message that you need to explore this relationship more deeply.

There are many types of care, an example of which is family day care – individualised small group care. Some families share a nanny, which can be cost-effective.

I have worked in the early childhood field for many years and have found the staff to be incredibly dedicated and willing to adapt programs and orientation for Sensitive children. Working with individual children's needs is, after all, their job. Communication with parents is a large part of the centre director's role, so ensure you have time to speak with them too.

Starting school

Many of us thrive on change, while others need careful leading and nurturing through new situations. I attended three primary schools and had a number of teachers; one each term for three years because I attended a small country primary school and teachers were difficult to recruit.

There were benefits of attending a small school for my supersensitivity. With 10 students in one room, the noise level was fairly low, so my anxiety about noise was mostly not a problem. When I moved to a much larger school and was in a class of 30 children, the story was very different. Initially, I was in trouble for talking as I had been used to discussing the work we were given, and often the teacher at the small school was working with other classes so we were left to our own devices.

Table 3. Transitions: childcare, kindergarten, school

- Have a prepared list for teaching staff of your child's favourite foods, security items or any other things that might be critical for helping your child settle in.

- Make sure you are feeling comfortable about your choice of centre, as your Sensitive child will pick up on any concerns or anxieties you have.

- Be prepared to stay for extended periods if your child is not settling well. Work out a strategy for leaving the centre with your child's carer or teacher and be prepared to vary it if it is not working.

- If you are supersensitive, talk to the teachers beforehand to make sure you are reassured and then use that information to talk to your child prior to them commencing.

- Make sure you talk about childcare, kindergarten or school in a positive way so that if your child hears any discussion, they will be feeling positive too.

- Try to meet other parents and children beforehand if possible. Creating social opportunities for your child outside of care or kindergarten will help them to transition.

- You can familiarise your child with their new childcare, kindergarten or school by walking past in the weeks before starting and pointing out things of interest to them.

- Many centres will encourage bringing a security item from home to leave in your child's bag in case they need it.

A guide for teachers

A teacher's role is incredibly complex. Faced with 23 or more new children each year including observing individual learning styles, covering a complex and large curriculum, supporting friendships and dealing with day-to-day stressors families deal with, it is not surprising that some children fall between the cracks.

The Australian curriculum is based on the premise of literacy and numeracy development with children as young as four years of age starting reading programs sometimes before they are developmentally ready. While this doesn't apply to all schools, literacy is a major focus in the early years of primary school. Some advanced children are ready for this formal learning but a large cohort are not.

This leads to children feeling stressed and parents concerned that they are not meeting milestones. One of the challenges for teachers and children is the physical structure of many classrooms and the formal nature of our current teaching, which requires children to sit at tables, or on a mat, listening for long periods of time. Children who are supersensitive have a particular need to use their creativity and sensory skills to learn, so a talk and chalk teaching style does not suit them, and can lead to a very stressed child. They also need to be able to use senses such as touch to help them to retain information. I find a stress ball particularly helpful when I am reading and trying to take in complex information. Visual prompts such as pictures also assist with learning.

Multisensory structured language is an approach now used by many teachers as a tool to support children with different learning styles. This is particularly useful for Sensitive children.

Sitting still is also difficult for many children and particularly for a Sensitive child who is sensitive to the energy of others around them. I am a right brain learner, highly creative and very sensitive to subtleties around me. I remember feeling sick, sad or fidgety when I sat next to certain children.

Aron talks about the ability of these children to tune into others' feelings and to notice subtleties other children don't. I feel that a great majority of supersensitives are right brain learners and being a right brain learner in a very structured environment can be incredibly stressful when feeling the pressure to conform to formal learning structures with little room for creativity.

> *Characteristics of right brain learners: take notes*
> *but lose them, have a hard time staying organized,*
> *struggle to make decisions (want to keep taking in more*
> *information before deciding), make friends easily and*
> *considered a people person, easily understand humour,*
> *seem dreamy but really deep thinking.*[8]

Education in other countries

In Finland and Sweden, the starting age for formal learning is seven. Children are given a creative, play-based early years curriculum until they start school.

Singapore known for high academic success also has a school starting age of seven.

Norway is currently trialling a later start for boys who often struggle with more formal learning. This will mean that many girls will start before boys who are not developmentally ready, but studies show that boys catch up in later years.[9] This is being trialled as there is a perception that boys are labelled as slow learners, when this not an accurate determination of their real skills.

Norway's former Education Minister, Sanner, commented that he was concerned many boys get poorer grades and end up dropping out to a greater degree than girls. He was not concerned that girls do well, but that schools get better at helping boys do better too.[10]

My observations indicate that educational experiences of not being ready for formal learning can be mirrored in the lives of supersensitive children as they take in much more information than their non-Sensitive peers. The overwhelm experienced by supersensitives sometimes leads teachers to conclude that they have ADHD or other learning difficulties when they really need to be supported with quiet learning environments and have a play-based curriculum catering to their right brain preferences until they're ready for more formal learning.

Highly sensitive children are easily bothered by things other children do not notice, and can become totally overwhelmed by a noisy complex constantly changing situation, like a classroom or a family reunion, especially if they are in that environment for too long.[11]

Aron also comments that as they are in the minority, their reactions and solutions often seem odd to others.

Other sensations they may be irritated by include being too hot or too cold and the environment being too noisy. Smells and light can also overstimulate them. They may have reactions such as being extremely active or overly upset, sometimes leading to a diagnosis of ADHD or sensory processing disorder. Neither of these is accurate for these children and as Aron says, what is a normal genetically inherited trait should not be labelled as a disorder.[12]

With the increased recognition of Sensitives, the development of these often-gifted children, needs to be catered for in the classroom. Sometimes they are medically labelled as overly sensitive. Many professionals with a medical background have tended to think of sensitivity as a disorder and as Aron notes in *The Highly Sensitive Child* that often therapists and professionals working with children tend to think of oversensitivity as a problem to be overcome or treated. I believe from my work with Sensitive children, as does Aron, that sensitivity is not a problem to be treated but as a personality trait to be considered as part of the spectrum of normal development.[13]

She does not deny that occupational therapy can help some Sensitives with lack of balance, coordination and stiffness but points out that these are normal issues for all children and some parents have also found it very useful for their Sensitive children.

Giftedness

From my 20-plus years of teaching and working with Sensitives, I have come to the conclusion that they are often either gifted overall or in a particular area.

Often not wanting to stand out, they will do their best to blend in with the class. If they are not encouraged and recognised for their skills and knowledge, they may become either quarrelsome or withdrawn, giving the impression that they are poor students. Because the majority are right brain learners and the mostly left brain–focused teaching style is incredibly stressful and often boring for them, they will appear to switch off their senses. This zoning out is sometimes seen by teachers as inattention when in reality the student often knows the material or is just uninterested and unengaged.

One very bright Sensitive child I know was very excited to start school. She had been able to use her creativity at kindergarten, was amazingly articulate, socially extroverted and able to hold a stimulating conversation with adults. She was in a class with boisterous boys and a teacher who was struggling to manage the class. Often a wriggler when she was bored, and she was constantly asked to sit still and listen.

Blessed with an amazing memory she became concerned that the teacher didn't follow through with promises she made to children regarding turn-taking and activities. Being helpful and reminding the teacher of this meant she was regarded as a troublesome student. Her writing skills were poor and she took a long time to complete writing tasks, leading to the impression she was a slow learner. She sensed this and withdrew from class participation.

As she was becoming depressed and not wanting to attend school, her parents took her to a psychologist educator, who specialised in children with learning issues. He assessed her as gifted in three of seven learning domains, average in the others and recommended a change of school. At her new school she was allowed to stand up to do her work, snack and drink in the classroom and take time out when she became overstimulated. She is now finishing secondary school and is a highly competent learner, still a little quirky, a great athlete, funny, a leader and a great advocate for other students.

Jan Tober and Lee Carroll in *The Indigo Children* discuss a new group of children who are often gifted, sometimes have a sense of entitlement and seem like they have been here before because of their incredible knowledge. With special gifts in one or a number of areas, they may be incredibly talented athletes, scientists, inventors, artists and advocates for others and the planet.[14]

Kath McClosky in the same book also gives examples of indigo children who were labelled as difficult and failing at school; however, when tested had exceptionally high IQs in many areas. They had been subscribed Ritalin and Cylert, two of the premier drugs for ADHD, without success.[15] Because these children don't fit what has been considered as normal, the reaction is to medicate their specialness.

Doreen Virtue questions whether there are children that are being misdiagnosed as having ADHD rather than as being gifted. She lists the following characteristics to help identify whether a child is gifted. (Many of these characteristics are also in my checklist for identifying Sensitives.)

Table 4. Gifted?

- Has high sensitivity.
- Has excessive amounts of energy.
- Bores easily-may appear to have a short attention span.
- Requires emotionally stable and secure adults around them.
- Will resist authority if it's not democratically oriented.
- Has preferred ways of learning particularly in reading and maths.
- May become easily frustrated because they have big ideas but lack the resources or people to assist them in carrying these tasks to fruition.
- Learns from an exploratory level, resisting rote memory or just being a listener.
- Cannot sit still unless absorbed in something of their own interest.
- Is very compassionate: has many fears such as loss and death of loved ones.
- If they experience failure early, may give up and develop permanent learning blocks.[16]

The US National Foundation for Gifted and Creative Children concurs with Virtue that gifted children may sacrifice their creativity in order to belong.[17]

In the classroom

Often teachers will have identified Sensitives as having special gifts and will support them in the system as much as possible. The main challenge being an overloaded curriculum and a lack of resources available to support both the family and the child through all stages of education.

In most cases in Australia, we tend to teach to the middle group of children in classes, so those at either end of the class gradient can miss out on the challenge or support needed to develop ongoing positive educational experiences.

Table 5. Tips for teachers

- When you identify a Sensitive child in your classroom, and statistics say you will often have two or three each year, make sure the room has withdrawal spaces and activities for extension and or support when needed.

- Expect students to take responsibility for the management of their need for additional challenges by having extension and creative activities easily available. They may initially need prompts to use these.

- Parents will sometimes be reluctant to talk with you about their supersensitive child, particularly if they are supersensitives themselves, so have some questions about sensitivity ready for the initial parent interview.

- Parents want their child to have friends, so they will be reliant upon you to support them with suggestions, particularly in the early years of school.

- Supersensitives need quiet time and space, particularly when they become overstimulated, so will need you to help them settle and refocus. A bean bag and earphones can be useful in helping an overstimulated Sensitive calm themself.

- Supersensitives are highly empathetic and will understand their peers' needs; therefore, other children will be attracted to play with them. However, a supersensitive may appear fussy about their choice of friends and avoid non-Sensitive peers.

- If you are not a Sensitive, you will find your supersensitive student can be very helpful in letting you know what is really going on with some friendships, as their powers of observation are highly tuned to notice human interactions.

- Your supersensitive student will see when you are not being authentic, so be prepared as they may point out inconsistencies in your teaching or a perceived lack of fairness. This can be quite challenging for non-Sensitives when done in front of other students.

- We have found, in our family, sensory input such as writing numbers on a child's back with a finger can help them remember their numbers and assist with correcting number and letter reversal.

Chapter 6

Sensitive adolescents

Every generation has its trials and none more than our current teenagers. The changes in society, in education, work and families have been massive.

Earlier generations had different pressures; those of war and poverty, limited medical care, lack of education and shortened life expectancy. These still exist for many of those living in third world countries, while our first world young people deal with technology developments, social and societal pressures unimagined even two generations ago. Who could imagine a world connected by technology which enables us to converse face to face with those in other countries?

In contrast, my father born in 1917 – more than 100 years ago – was excited and amazed by the first air flight. His teenage years were ones of work, helping to support his parents and siblings get through a Depression where starvation was a real possibility. Leaving school at 14 to work rather than accept a scholarship meant the stresses he encountered were those of leaving family to work digging roads. He went on to be a farmer as his father before him had done. Our industrial laws today require young people to be almost 15 before they can work and 16 before they can leave school.

Conflict

Puberty is an incredible period of growth and change both physically emotionally and socially for all young people; particularly so if they are a supersensitive. Reflecting on my teenage years, not only were the changes to my body embarrassing I mostly wanted to ignore, but my emotions were also highly aroused much of the time. With limited understanding of my supersensitivity and intuitive nature, teenage years which could have been fun were often fraught with doubts about my intelligence, my artistic ability, my friends, my physical appearance, my weight and my possible romantic relationships with boys.

Usually a compliant and happy person, I found myself vehemently disagreeing with my father's ideas and we had some hot discussions about the state of the world, apartheid, the contraceptive pill, war, and my lack of freedom to go out with friends. Highly sensitive to criticism and negative comments, I would react angrily to my parents when they were critical of my friends or conversely praised them for undertaking activities they really wanted me to do. My supersensitive nature could see right through this and often I would try to avoid mealtimes knowing an argument could ensue.

Conflict usually makes me run for cover but in those mid-teenage years I found myself questioning everything, having arguments with my father and worrying I would not cope as an adult. Hypersensitive to criticism I can still feel the hurt and anxiety present when compared academically with others. I am sure it is part of the reason I have been a part-time student for about 18 years... plus six years full time... when will enough be enough?

My cousin, who was the same age, lived with us for a six-month period when I was 13. We shared a bedroom for this time and as a Sensitive, I found this extremely stressful. The noise, the lack of time alone and sharing my precious personal things all added to the daily concerns of suddenly having to accommodate another teenager sharing my space. Highly sensitive to smells I used to flinch and gag when she took her shoes off!

I was reminded of this recently when driving my granddaughter home from school. She screwed up her nose and asked what the smell was in my car. I realised I had eaten a fish cake for lunch and the container was still in the car in a plastic bag but her Sensitive's nose had picked it up.

The sound of my cousin's breathing was also enough to keep me tossing and turning for hours. So too would my maths and sports results when compared with hers. Looking back now I can see that it was my dad's way of building her confidence as she was going through an extremely stressful time with her family. My parents were worried I might become spoilt as I was an only child for nearly eight years until my brother arrived.

Being highly creative, sensitive and spirited was not valued during my school years.

What the evidence says

Adolescence is known to be an anxious and stressful time for many young people. A host of changes to the body, fast growth spurts, raging hormones, moral development forming, academic, parental and peer pressure increasing, and the brain developing at a rapid rate. All of these challenges, plus add a teenager who is a Sensitive and trying to make sense of the world.

Cheryl Feinstein in *Secrets of the Teenage Brain*[18] discusses the brain research which now indicates that neuroscience tells us it is not hormones that are the major culprit for adolescent anxiety but rather the ever-changing brain processes which are destroying old neutral connections and building new pathways.

Feinstein says this will alter how parents and teachers interpret teenage behaviour. These brain changes are often played out in emotional outbursts and angry and often irrational behaviour.

Add extreme sensitivity to this mix and parents and teachers can see why some children – particularly those in the 15 to 20% – have enormous stress and angst during this time.

Decision making and risk taking

Feinstein further espouses that it is unrealistic to expect teenagers to exhibit the same problem-solving ability as an adult. While in the past we have looked at risk taking as part of a rite of passage and part of the growing up process particularly during puberty, decision making involves a number of processes. Adults use prior knowledge coupled with experience of similar situations, values and moral code. For teenagers, these are all in the process of formulating. They are navigating a changing brain and body, as well as the nature of their relationships within their family, with their teachers and with their peers.[19]

Risk taking in many guises often forms part of the development of many teenagers. This, coupled with peer pressure, the ever-changing technological world and the easy access to drugs and alcohol all add to the pressure. The limits of previous generations no longer apply to most young people but have been replaced with different concerns.

Stable employment, affordable tertiary education and an economy where the opportunity to purchase and own a house or flat are diminishing for this generation of teenagers who may also have shorter life spans then their parents due to increasing pollution and corrupted food supplies. Sensitives are likely to absorb many of the societal concerns about these and other issues.

Chapter 7

Sensitives and psychic abilities

We are a society committed to labels for explaining behaviours which don't fit the norm – whatever they are.

Our acceptance of the inexplicable and esoteric is limited to our spirituality based primarily on Christian values which often limit rather than embrace psychic phenomena.

We also generally believe that wisdom comes with age and that the young need to absorb this as they grow.

What if there was much more than we are able to see and understand, and the children being born now come with more knowledge and wisdom than previous generations? A radical notion for some and I realise will not be one which will be embraced by everyone. If you find it doesn't resonate with you then I suggest you skip this chapter.

I had an experience with my granddaughter Poppy aged two and a half, who described how she came to Earth for me. We were driving in the car and she commented on things which happened before she was born, these were things she could not have possibly known. Needless to say, I was very surprised, but have since heard many parents and grandparents share similar stories.

When in the United Kingdom, I was once again very surprised when a clairvoyant onstage had a message for me from a father and son who had both died. The message was a thank you for the work I had done with a little boy 25 years earlier, when working with terminally ill children. The clairvoyant described the songs from his funeral and other activities we had done.

In our family it is common to feel or see energy; for me this manifests as strong prickly type feelings and sometimes if the energy is negative I may feel nauseous. Two of my granddaughters see auras or the human energy field, describing them as seeing rainbows around people or people in colour. When my father was dying, our family stayed with him until he passed. The great grandchildren aged five and three were present, talking with him and saying goodbye.

Three-year-old Brigitta was drawing. The drawings were put aside as everyone was focused on saying goodbye, organising the funeral, eulogy and videos. Later when I reviewed the drawings, it was obvious she had drawn the family. Grandfarmer, as the children called him, in bed with an energy stream going from the bed to the roof; this drawing illustrated the ability to see energy. She could see this, which was not obvious to others in the room. Children often report seeing angels and auras. People who are present with the dying often report seeing light at the time of death.

The human energy field can also often be seen by clairvoyants, reiki practitioners and other healers. There are many reports of people in the presence of the dying noticing visible changes of energy and light in the room as a person passes over. Beatle George Harrison's wife Olivia described:

> *There was a profound experience that happened when he left*
> *his body. It was visible, let's just say, you wouldn't need to light*
> *the room, if you were trying to film it. He just ... lit the room.*[20]

So, what does this mean for parents and teachers?

The issues involved here are those of belief and appropriate responses to psychic or clairvoyant experiences. Children need validation and acceptance; they need to be believed. As a teacher or parent, it is important you listen even if you can't see or feel anything.

Lisa Williams, in her book *The Survival of the Soul,* discusses playing with friends only she could see, and her parents not believing her. I had the same experience with my pretend friends (spirit children), Did and Dodd. My parents let me talk about them but I am not sure they believed me, so I soon learned not to discuss our adventures.

*When your Sensitive child talks about seeing dead people,
or just seeing other people or children that are not visible
to you, don't deny their experience.*

If they are having bad dreams, it may in fact be people who have passed over visiting them. You can explain to them that it's okay to tell the Universe that they don't have to accept these experiences and they would like them to be turned off.

Tips for parents and teachers

Table 6. Dealing with psychic abilities

- Listen to your child and take what they say seriously, even if you are a non-believer.
- Ensure they have a night light in their room.
- Tell them they can stop people visiting them by asking the Universe to switch off these people.
- Acknowledge them when they ask to be moved away from other students in the classroom because of the energy they can feel.
- Often able to feel their peers' feelings, they may become irritated and fidgety when it is another child who is feeling upset, and need to find a safe space away from others until they feel less anxious.
- Have coping strategies worked out with them such as having a bean bag in the library area they can withdraw to.
- Provide them with earplugs to block out overwhelming noises and other peoples' voices.

Chapter 8

Maximising friendships

Friendships form the foundation for a happy life. Understanding another and being understood are fundamental needs for most humans. Indeed, they are what makes us human.

Nothing is more heartbreaking for me than a child coming home in tears stating: "I have no friends." This happened with both of my Sensitive children when they first started school and again later when we moved to the country and they changed schools. Until this happened, I hadn't put much thought into analysing it from a family perspective. I was then challenged to intervene and support them. But how to do this without firstly undermining their confidence and being immediately labelled as an interfering mum?

When working with children and their families, I have observed that a difficult educational situation can be made bearable through having great friendships. This is particularly so for Sensitive children, as they are keen to understand and connect with others, often through their energy and feelings.

I have observed that Sensitive children often demonstrate high empathy and can interpret the behaviour of their classmates as either being open to friendships or not. This may mean that they do not approach children they sense will not respond well to friendship requests judging them to being too boisterous or not open to new friendships. It may also mean that they miss out on possible friendships and activities because of this. Sensitives can also worry about rejection, therefore, sometimes it is easier to choose to play alone.

Personality also has an impact. Some personality types are more outgoing and find approaching and making friends easy. The personality traits of extroversion and introversion have an impact on the making and keeping of friendships.

Extroversion and introversion

Aron in her research found Sensitive children at both ends of the spectrum for extroversion, which perhaps seems counterintuitive. Approximately 60% were high introverts and 40% high extroverts.[21] Both of these traits have their challenges for parents.

A Sensitive child who is introverted may be reluctant to approach other children and indeed lack the skills to engage others in play. Highly extroverted children can become dispirited when using their intuition as they have amazing ideas for games. Their enthusiasm may not be shared by their non-Sensitive peers who don't necessarily see the fun in what their friend is proposing, particularly if it includes complicated rules and is risky.

In my experience, Sensitive children are incredibly creative when it comes to making up games and extroverted Sensitive children are often comfortable with a high level of risk.

Friendships at school

In my teaching years, matching children with possible friends was part of my work. Somehow, I just knew who would have common interests, energy levels and who would have a shared understanding. I would suggest to parents who could undertake play dates, and who would be great in class together when starting school. I knew the Prep teachers at the local primary schools and spent time doing transition work with my kindergarten children to ensure school was a good first experience.

Looking back, I now realise that making friends was an issue I struggled with as a child and now it was emerging once again for our children. My children's father also had similar issues; I'm sure he is a Sensitive too.

The tone of a school is highly influenced by its leadership and I have observed principals who leave intervention regarding bullying or disruptive behaviour until the last minute, and others who ensure fast action, so that students have very clear boundaries in the playground.

Sensitive children are often particularly good at avoiding trouble because of their ability to predict events. This can mean that they self-isolate and don't join groups due to a fear of criticism, getting the rules of the game wrong or getting into trouble.

Some actively avoid competition, particularly if it means drawing attention to themselves. Alternatively, extroverted Sensitives can become querulous if they think other students or teachers are not treating everyone in the playground fairly.

My granddaughter is an amazing gymnast with a natural ability to move her body in a most poetic way. She also has a steely determination to practise and work at a routine until she is satisfied it is perfect. She sometimes chooses to play alone or sit quietly under a tree rather than be with other children. The time alone helps her recharge away from the noisy classroom. She also chooses to be friends with boys in her class as they are interested in similar things and fortunately, she is attending a school where this is encouraged.

When she competed in her first gym competition, she admonished her dad for posting her routine on Facebook and had him take it down immediately, stating she was doing this for herself. Sensitive children often suffer embarrassment from being the centre of attention and experience these feelings much more keenly than their peers.

When our children moved schools from a large multicultural inner-Melbourne school to a much smaller, less culturally diverse country school, they both struggled making friends. Fortunately, their grandparents knew some families who lived locally and they introduced our daughter to two girls who were in the same grade and she eventually played with them. She was a tomboy, so she made friends with boys too. Two of her best friends were boys, both Sensitives, and they supported her when she was bullied by a group of girls.

Our son had issues whereby while he was friendly, he was extremely introverted and took time to find his feet. On the other hand, he had the confidence and foresight to suggest to his new teacher that she could telephone the teacher at his other school for interesting ideas of things to do in the afternoon. He was very bored and thought this would help! The teacher was not very receptive to his great idea, which didn't help their relationship.

Labelled as difficult because of his impertinence, his Prep year was not a happy one in class; the playground was a happier story. We had introduced him to a family of boys who lived nearby and travelled on the same bus. One of those boys, also a Sensitive, became one of his best friends. Although a year older and in another class, they played together, had sleepovers and had common interests which led to many adventures.

When your child is one of the few Sensitives in the class, finding a friend who understands them is a challenge.

You may need to help them find a friend in another year level.

A feature of my childhood, my sensitivity led me to hang out with a boy who liked animals, frogs, tadpoles and lizards. He was the only one at the small school I attended with whom I resonated. I was often bullied and teased because I played with boys and, because of my extroverted sensitivity, would give my opinion in class only to be categorised as a smarty pants. When I clicked with a teacher, I did very well. If I did not like or respect the teacher, I would zone out and do the minimum of work.

Bullying

Bullying is often part of Sensitive children's school experience. My children and grandchildren have all experienced some form of bullying during their school experience. This has been dealt with in different ways at their schools. Some had programs which helped students accept difference, and built this into the curriculum. However, often there is the feeling that students will work it out themselves.

Sensitive children do not want to stand out, so will often resist parents who want to take the situation further. You know your child well, so don't be afraid to intervene and work with teachers to improve the situation.

Social media is a complex area as often subtle bulling is away from parents' scrutiny. A group chat which may seem friendly can be very subtle and damaging to a child who is being excluded. Often girls will encourage one another to share secrets and if the relationship changes, these can be used against the excluded child in unkind and damaging ways, aimed to hurt and undermine confidence.

Teenagers

As supersensitives, Sensitive teenagers are mostly very empathetic and good listeners, friends and sometimes adults will share their problems or fears and even secrets with them. This is particularly concerning for one of my granddaughters who holds special secrets for friends sometimes causing her sleepless nights. She is now able to discuss these concerns with a parent who can advise her how to deal with these issues.

Aron offers the advice that ensuring your teenager is able to share concerns with a trusted person is important so that they do not have to keep worries and events to themselves.[22] Also let them know that it is okay to put some boundaries around the sharing of feelings and personal information.

Personality plays a role here too as those who have a preference for introversion will not find sharing feelings or talking at any time helpful. In addition, while teenagers share on social media, a face-to-face discussion with a parent can seem too intrusive .

Children and teenagers today use technology such as smart phones, social media and online gaming to connect with one another. Particularly since the advent of COVID-19, young people have depended upon social media and technology to remain in contact. The way they use it may be different to the way adults will use it to connect with one another. Phone calls are a thing of the past; instead messages written and recorded will be sent to dozens if not hundreds of people at a time. This can lead to issues and anxiety when responses as expected are not forthcoming, particularly for Sensitive children. Apps like Snapchat and Instagram have created a culture that desires "followers", "views" and "likes" as a way of validating one's popularity or desirability.

There are also many positive aspects to the use of technology for the connection of young people, particularly the ability to connect to like-minded people who may not live locally or even within the same country.

Supersensitive children, particularly those who are introverted, can find making friends online less stressful than face to face. There is a need, though, for parental support in monitoring usage.

Table 7. Supporting Sensitives to make friends

- Make sure the school has support mechanisms in place to support children's playground relationships.

- I know of a state primary school that has a Friendship Tree. Students lacking friends go to the tree and other students are encouraged to help them join in their group. If students are seen there, often their teacher and the deputy principal step in to assist. This also has the impact of giving students some responsibility in helping peers.

- A project implemented in a rural area initially for Indigenous children included a structure with a seat and a totem pole, which was unveiled by the community as a safe place for students who felt overwhelmed or unable to cope in the classroom to retreat to, instead of running away from school.

- Many schools are now working with a Buddy system and older children support Prep or younger children, both in the classroom and in the playground.

- Check to see if your school encourages families to meet before school begins. Many schools have a parent welcoming group which enables parents and new students to get together before school starts. A friendly face on that first day will make all the difference to this new adventure for your Sensitive child.

- Make sure you have time with the teacher one-on-one to discuss your child's sensitivity. Having written information about any special food or interests will assist the teacher in their teaching role. Information about sensitivity and how it presents in your child can also help support your child's friendship experiences.

- Make an effort to get to know other parents. You will soon learn who may have a child who resonates with your Sensitive.

- Be prepared for your child to take their time to find friends and that they might need your support for a longer time than other children. Confidently discuss your issues with their teacher and ask them for support if your child is having issues. Often your child will not be the only one needing support in those first few weeks.

- If your child is truly miserable and the school is not responding, is there the option of another school for your child? Research about the types of activities, curriculum, parental support and involvement can help guide you to make the correct decision.

- Have a system for monitoring your child's social media so that you can monitor their communication with peers and other friends. Don't be afraid to check in on group chats as it is a safety issue, as well as a way to send a message to your child that unacceptable comments will be noticed and dealt with.

Chapter 9

Anxiety and depression

Butterflies in my stomach have always been there and now I have the means to identify and tame them. It was not always so. When I was little, I appeared to be confident and very active; I was sometimes called "the Little Wind" as I ran from one adventure to another. Now I know more about extroverted Sensitive children and the effects of anxiety, this response now make sense.

> *Sensitive children can sometimes be labelled as hyperactive. However, careful management of these children can reduce their anxiety to such a degree that they are able to concentrate for long periods, engage well with their peers and perform well in classroom activities. Reducing classroom stimulation both visual and auditory can be very effective in reducing distractions for extroverted Sensitives.*

Boredom or lacking engagement with the teacher can lead to oppositional and disruptive behaviour. Primary classrooms which enable children to move around freely and to choose their workspaces and activities cater well for Sensitive children. I have known children who constantly need to move, responding well to standing to do their work. Snacks and water also help with the jiggling.

I was one of these children, and was constantly getting into trouble for getting up from my desk and moving due to sensory overload because of the noisy environment. Concentration was difficult because I was highly aware of sounds, smells, movement and other conversations taking place.

Being alone in the dark was always frightening. My earliest part-memory was being in my cot and crying and no one coming for a very long time.

It was a time when I was being cared for by my father's aunt who had no children of her own and limited experience with any babies, so it was probably exacerbated by the absence of my mother.

Attachment styles

All of us have different types of attachment styles which impact on how we interact with others. Formed in the first year of life, this refers to the mental picture of what we expect of our caregivers and others. Aron states that 40% of adults have an insecure attachment style and Sensitives are affected more adversely when poor attachment occurs.[22] As parents, our own experience influences how we parent, so parents with an insecure style tend to raise children who are also insecure.

Awareness of your attachment style can assist you with parenting your Sensitive. Supersensitive children need parents or caregivers who are very responsive and switched on to the child's needs. An anxious or avoidant attachment style will be extremely stressful for your highly sensitive child. Non-Sensitive children, however, can manage a range of reactions and behaviours from their parents and caregivers. A mother's responsiveness and attachment in the first years of life has a major impact on not only how children deal with stressful situations but on their relationship choices later in life. Try to minimise stress in the first years of a supersensitive child's life by limiting the times they are separated from main caregivers

My granddaughter did not cope with separation from her parents for any length of time with either new or unfamiliar caregivers. On two occasions, when she was left with a grandparent and/or babysitter she cried for the two hours her mother was absent, not letting anyone comfort her. The babysitter bought her favourite cake the next time but it made no difference, she still cried herself to sleep beside the front door. Needless to say, leaving her with unfamiliar people was not an option.

Overstimulation

When we moved to a farm, I became adept at finding my way when outside in the dark but the fears of the darkness continued when I was inside, particularly when in my bedroom. Particularly sensitive to noise, I often woke to the sound of the tree in the wind or a possum on the roof. I haven't outgrown this but have learned to manage it with meditation and keeping a pet inside.

My grandchildren use several strategies to deal with anxieties of the night: night lights, a parent sitting beside the bed, back rubs, sleeping with parents as toddlers and pre-schoolers, special blankets and toys.

As children grow, they learn mostly acceptable strategies to manage their anxieties. These can vary and I have seen some children carry their special soothers, which in attachment behaviour theory would indicate that first soothers such as security blankets are initially a replacement for the primary caregiver – usually Mum. I have observed that children who have trouble settling often need particular rituals which assist them with sleeping.

Our western culture, which often stimulates children all day with devices, games, loud noises, conversation and constant activity, does not support easily settling. It is customary for babies in the Netherlands, for instance, to be kept at home in a routine without the sort of outings we take our babies to. The evidence indicates that they respond well to this calm and sheltered environment by exhibiting excellent sleeping habits.[23]

We often expect newborns to be handed around to extended family and friends – something very stressful to an introverted Sensitive baby, less so for the 80% of non-Sensitives.

When managing a mothers and babies hospital specialising in sleeping support, it was very obvious to me that a sleep program developed for babies who had difficulty sleeping was not suitable for some babies, particularly those Sensitives. Some of the routines and strategies led to a baby and parent who were more stressed. Once again, I would encourage parents to use their own inner guidance, listen to advice, but know when to accept or reject it as being suitable for your child.

Teen and pre-teen and anxiety

What about those teen and pre-teen years; how do we as parents deal with school transitions, puberty and life in general?

As an extroverted Sensitive teen, I suffered from a constant internal dialogue of criticism and doubt about my scholastic achievements – a dilemma regarding the opinions of my friends versus those of my parents (something all teenagers go though, I hear you say), but this internal dialogue did not seem to be as loud as my class colleagues.

I was known for talking in class – never popular behaviour with teachers – but discussing issues with classmates helped me to learn. In an era where students were supposed to listen and rarely give their opinion, I struggled to stay engaged, particularly if the subject seemed to have little relevance for my future. My favourite subjects were science, biology and art.

Great teachers who encouraged and inspired me even when I didn't believe in myself helped me manage my anxiety. Nerves always played a big part in how I performed in exams. At that time, all assessment for Years 11 and 12 was done by three-hour examinations, marked externally from the school. The only student in my year to pass all six subjects in Year 11, I then bombed out spectacularly in Year 12 due to anxiety. I remember vomiting before each exam and the pounding in my head made it almost impossible to think.

Repeating Year 12 and feeling a total failure I then went on to college and university where I was able to study in many areas. I think anxiety regarding assessment is a common theme for Sensitives and it is fortunate that academic assessment is now not only based on examinations but progressively on the total year's work.

> *Social situations and friendships for Sensitive teens are often times full of grief for both parents and children. Social media compounds this with both the fear of missing out and slights, real or imagined, being incredibly stressful for Sensitives.*

Bullying is also a challenge and can be subtle and not obvious to teachers and parents but debilitating for the young person. There are many examples of young people dealing with bullying alone, leading to tragic outcomes.

Stress

In this era of social media, teenagers have never been so in touch with the world and everyday news events. Even if parents monitor and restrict the use of technology, their peers are informed about what is happening and therefore avoiding bad news is almost impossible.

Social media also plays a big part in how teenagers form their opinions about how society treats those who may be viewed as being different.

This year has been unprecedented in terms of stress with COVID-19 sweeping the world. We don't know what impact this will have on the long-term mental health of the world's nations or our children. My eight-year-old grandson has been very worried about what would happen if I caught the virus and has been super-vigilant about staying away from people and following the rules. His 17-year-old sister gets extremely nervous and upset when she sees people depicted in the media not following the rules.

The impact of supersensitivity and stress has been discussed earlier in the information regarding genes and we know that Sensitive individuals have different stress reactions to their non-Sensitive peers.

The recent plebiscite on gay marriage in Australia has opposing groups brought into stark view. This has not been helpful in espousing and enacting equality in Australian society. Sadly, it has been used to attack gay people and to use religious zealotry to criticise and bully those with differing views. In a free and democratic society all views need to be respected and be respectful; however, some have chosen to aggressively attack others. Teenagers who are still exploring their sexuality are particularly vulnerable to these types of attacks. Sensitive teenagers more so, as they are hardwired to take in and feel others' pain.

I am aware of young people rewriting their Facebook pages, even changing their names, after the bullying and vitriol from others not supporting gay marriage caused them enormous stress.

Recently, someone shared with me their family story whereby the pain of telling his parents he was gay was relived because of this plebiscite, as his parents had voted no to gay marriage. As the healer in the family, and the one most committed to supporting his parents as they age, he now feels disrespected and unsupported once again. Now in his forties and supersensitive, he told his story of coming out as a teenager and how he had been depressed for many years, choosing to live a distance away from his parents in order to become independent. Family and contact with his siblings used to give him much joy, but now he chooses to have little contact with them as the criticism continues.

Another Sensitive teenager I know at the age of 13 is considering her sexuality. Highly intelligent and engrossed in thinking about philosophical questions not pondered by most adults, she has expressed fear for the future of the planet and is not sure she wants to be here. She has a family where at least one parent is quite controlling, disrespectful and outspoken about difference and family disagreement is the norm, so it is very difficult to express her needs. With counselling and family support she is considering her options. Apart from the challenge of a school which can support and test her amazing intellect, one of her main worries is how to find friends who understand her.

I know from experience that being supersensitive and intuitive, finding friends who do not seem too harsh in their opinions has always been something I am painfully aware of. I could not relate to the girl groups who were almost gang-like in their operations and usually found ways to bully others.

One day in Year 6 stands out. As a new kid at the school, I was eager to find friends. Incredibly naïve and trusting I was adopted by the gang. My joy soon turned to shock when they cornered me and twanged my bra strap, made sexual comments about my developing body and warned me to stay away from their boyfriends. Being a farm kid, I had been at a school of 10 students until Year 6. Now confronted with 600 students, keeping my head down and surviving was a priority. Luckily for me I found two girls who were best friends and they adopted me as their project.

We all went to high school together and then teachers' college. Although I don't see much of them now, we can meet after a few years and still get each other. I am sure we are all supersensitive.

Suicide

The incidence of depression and anxiety in supersensitive individuals has been documented in a new book about high sensitivity, *The Orchid and the Dandelion* by W Thomas Boyce[24] and in Aron's aforementioned book *The Highly Sensitive Child*. Boyce documents his supersensitive sister's journey into anorexia and comments at how the lack of understanding of her anxiety and other mental health issues contributed to her further decline.

There are documented examples in the media of young people being bullied on social media and the devastating consequences. In many of these examples, the parents commented on the supersensitivity of these individuals. They also make the observation that their child hid their distress very well.

As a Sensitive I have experienced depression and anxiety and at a very low time in my life, contemplated suicide. My family and friends were not aware of what was happening to me and there was no way I was going to tell them about feeling like a complete failure. Alone and going through a divorce in another state away from my usual networks, my isolation was adding to my distress.

At an incredibly low ebb, I sought the help of a counsellor and became aware of how potent my sensitivity and anxiety were. Dealing with it has made a big difference and has enabled me to become a more empathetic and spiritual person since realising that I am not alone.

I have found meditation, contemplation and retreats, where I can stop and recalibrate and tune into what I really want in my professional and personal life, incredibly helpful for managing my anxiety.

Considering social media has been blamed for the escalating deaths of young people, what might be the other issues influencing this trend?

In *Raising a Screen-Smart Kid*, Julianna Miner discusses an example of an 11-year-old girl who is trolled by a predator. Eighteen months of communication took place before her family discovered the online communications. She suffered severe depression and a suicide attempt.[25]

Sensitive children are sometimes more vulnerable to depression and anxiety, particularly if they are isolated from peers due to their uniqueness.

If they are introverted, online friendships can appear to be easier if the only contact is online. However, there is mounting evidence that the more people use social media, the worse they feel, impacting greatly on their wellbeing and mental health. For Sensitive children exhibiting anxiety, there need to be limits in place to help them manage their usage and reactions to negative information.

Managing Sensitive teens

Table 8. Managing Sensitive teens

- Make time to talk with your child even when they avoid you or don't have much to say.

- I have found that having a culture of sharing at mealtime – even when there is resistance – is helpful with children in their teen years.

- Warning signs can be incredibly subtle and often attributed to teenage moodiness (very real), so learning to read between the lines is important for parents.

- Keep in touch with the school and make sure they are aware if your child is struggling.

- Teenagers will often cover their social media interactions very cleverly, but a culture of checking social media such as Facebook combined with discussions about the pitfalls need to begin when they are just starting with social media, so they are less resistant to it as they get older.

- Have boundaries around the use of technology and make sure you are clear and confidently implement them.

- Put the rules in writing and then display them in a place visible to everyone.

- Use timers, apps and parental control for agreed upon time limits. Give the child responsibility to monitor their own behaviour.

- Set the example for them by sticking to your own rules.

- Adequate sleep is extremely important to Sensitive children, so ensure technology time is limited well before bed, which allows them time to wind down.

Chapter 10

Sensitives and allergies

Food allergies

The number of children presenting to children's hospitals with allergies has been steadily increasing. At the Royal Children's Hospital, Melbourne we have experienced increased demand for allergic disease care. For example, hospital admissions for anaphylactic patients have increased three-fold in just five years.[26]

One of the questions I have pondered is whether a higher sample of these children are supersensitive and are more of these children being born? Anecdotally speaking with parents, teachers and maternal and child health nurses, this seems to be the case, but I do not have the answer. A research project in this area would give more clarity to this question.

My familial experience appears to bear out this theory but I feel more research needs to be done in this area. I am unsure of the genetic links but know my grandfather, my father and myself all had negative reactions to some foods, such as oranges. So, when our son was diagnosed with a sucrose intolerance and could not tolerate cane sugar or other sugars, this did not come as a surprise.

Dr Margaret Smith with Sue Williams discuss the genetic influences of food intolerances and the evolution of gene mutations which are the blueprint for our genetic inheritance. For example, in terms of lactose intolerance, they state that only 35% of the global population is able to digest lactose.[27] How does this tie in with the supersensitivity of some children or are there no links at all?

Asthma and eczema

Asthma is a chronic inflammatory disease of the airways.[28]

Apart from food intolerances, asthma, eczema and other skin allergies are increasing.

Parents I have worked with often report that their supersensitive child has asthma and other allergic reactions such as hives. I am allergic to drugs such as penicillin and my father had severe reactions to aspirin and other pain medication. This presented as swelling of the face and airways. Bee and ant stings cause the same reaction in two of my supersensitive friends.

Once again, more questions than answers. Does supersensitivity come with added medical or health challenges, or are medical and health challenges increasing expedientially in the population?

There are many resources for managing these health issues on the internet and discussions with health professionals will support your child in managing them. Many parents I have spoken with also find alternative medicine helpful for managing their children's anxiety and fears about their supersensitive reactions to new and unfamiliar situations.

In conclusion, if your supersensitive child finds that everyday activities and life in general presents you both with problems to be solved, be assured there is help, recognition and resources to assist with reducing their anxieties, making sense of their quirkiness and celebrating their differences. Life with a supersensitive will never be dull and most days will be delightfully different and surprising.

Frequently asked questions

I am not sure if my child is a Sensitive or at times just being difficult to get attention. My other children don't behave like him.

The checklist in Chapter 1 regarding elements of sensitivity will give you an indication of whether your child is a supersensitive. Elaine Aron's online checklist can be used as well.[29]

In my experience, children want to cooperate when they are being heard and respected.

Sensitive children, when overstimulated, can have quite strong outbursts, surprising themselves and their parents.

Sensitives usually want to fit in, so will usually not unnecessarily draw attention to themselves.

My child is usually cooperative but he gets very upset when we laugh at something funny he has said or done.

Sensitive children feel things more intensely and can see laughter as criticism rather than as encouraging or supportive.

Try to put yourself in his shoes and explain that the laughter was supposed to be friendly.

Remember, if you are not being truthful, supportive or authentic then he will know and lose respect for you.

My daughter loves going to stay with her grandparents but does not like sleeping in their guest room. She asks to sleep on the floor of their bedroom. The other grandchildren are all happy to sleep in the guest room, so it is an awkward situation.

Sensitive children are very sensitive to smells, sounds and energy, and sometimes see things other non-Sensitives don't.

Talk about the reasons she does not want to sleep in that particular room.

Sometimes a night light will help. Taking her own bedding may help.

For example, I am particularly sensitive to smells and try to take my own pillow and doona with me in new situations.

My child's school has a school camp for Year 3 children away from the school for two nights. I am concerned about the sleepover aspect as she has never been for a sleepover except with family and she is sensitive.

Sleepovers are often very stressful for Sensitive children.

Speak with the teacher to ensure they are prepared.

If possible, ask for friends to be placed together and give your child reassurance that the teacher is on hand if they are worried.

If it will be too stressful for your child then it may be best for them to stay home.

My baby seems to startle more easily than the other babies in the mothers' group and she also cries more. Other parents can put their babies down to sleep with everyone around but my baby screams if I put her down where it's noisy.

Sensitive babies have a more highly sensitive nervous system, so noise and unfamiliar sounds will be very unsettling to them.

You are your baby's best advocate: avoid comparisons and avoid situations where your child becomes overstimulated by the environment.

If she needs you to nurse her or feed her during the group meeting, it is time be confident to do so.

My eight-year-old has been spending a lot of time on devices during COVID-19 lockdown. He constantly asks for my phone, computer or iPad and refuses to go outside to play. It wears me down and to keep the peace I give in. I know I have to limit this but it's complex.

It is very hard to limit technology. As studies have shown it alters children's brains, with a similar addictive effect as heroin, and therefore it is important that you work out a system where his screen time is limited.

A wall chart with times and suggestions of other activities can be helpful.

Give him the responsibility of a timer so he is monitoring himself and have strict rules around usage.

It will be difficult at first but remember you are working with a strong influence, so it may take at least a month before habits change.

You also need to be aware how you model your own usage for him.

My five-year-old has food allergies and this gets complicated at birthday parties as well-meaning parents offering him food he should not be eating.

Talk to the parent having the party and let them know about the issue.

I found that with our son, he was quite capable of refusing lollies at parties because he knew how sick he became if he ate sugar.

Children are very used to having different food at childcare and kindergarten, so check out the food and put some things your child can eat on a different plate.

If it is too difficult to manage then you may need to stay at the party also.

My 15-year-old daughter is becoming more withdrawn and stays in her room more. She says everything is okay when I ask her. Should I be concerned?

Teenagers experience peer pressure, particularly through social media and can get caught up in bullying and online trolling.

If she is refusing to show you her phone, you need to find a way to address this as it may be an indication something more serious is going on for her.

Check in with the teacher and notice if her friendships have changed. Girls at this age can be particularly unkind and bully subtly by leaving their peer out and then posting their activities online.

Talk to her about this and encourage activities which help her to engage with other students. Sometimes friends outside of school can be helpful too.

Bibliography

Publications

Aron, E. N, *The Highly Sensitive Child.* (2002), Random House USA

Boyce, T., MD *The Orchid and the Dandelion: Why Sensitive People Struggle and How All Can Thrive.* (2019), Bluebird UK

Briggs, Myers, I., *Introduction to Type: A Guide to Understanding Your Results on the Myers-Briggs Type Indicator.* (2000) Oxford Psychologists Press, Oxford, 6th edition. Reprinted in Australia CPP Asia Pacific

Carroll, L. & Tobler, J., *The Indigo Children.* (1999), Hay House USA

Feinstein, S., *Secrets Of the Teenage Brain.* (2014), SAGE, USA

Miner, J., *Raising a Screen Smart Kid.* (2019), Penguin Random House LLC USA

Smith M., Dr & Williams, S., *Gene Genius.* (2015), Harlequin Non-fiction Australia

Websites

Daily Mail, Australia. "The dying light exploring the strange phenomenon of lights seen at the time of death." (May, 2020) www.dailygrail.com/2020/05/the-dying-light-exploring-the-strange-phenomenon-of-lights-seen-at-the-time-of-death/ Accessed 8 Feb 2021

Institute for Multisensory Structured Education www.multisensoryeducation.net.au Accessed 8 Feb 2021

News in English. "Norway to start to try a more flexible school start" by Nina Bergland. www.newsinenglish.no/2019/08/20/norway-to-try-more-flexible-school-start. Accessed Jan 2020

Royal Children's Hospital, Melbourne. Asthma fact sheet. www.rch.org.au/kidsinfo/fact_sheets/asthma/ Accessed 10 Feb 2021

Royal Children's Hospital, Melbourne. "Allergy & Immunology." blogs.rch.org.au/news/2007/05/31/allergy-services/ 25 May 2020. Accessed 9 Feb 2021

References

1 Briggs, Myers, I., *Introduction to Type: A Guide to Understanding Your Results on the Myers-Briggs Type Indicator* (2000), 6th edition. Revised by Linda K. Kirby, Katharine D. Myers. Oxford Psychologists Press, Oxford.

2 Aron E., *The Highly Sensitive Child.* (2002). Broadway Books, USA

3 Aron, E., Sensitive Child Checklist (Checklist available online see in references)

4 Aron op. cit.

5 Smith M., Dr & Williams, S., *Gene Genius.* (2015), Harlequin Non-fiction Australia

6 Smith M., Dr & Williams, S., *Gene Genius.* (2015), Harlequin Non-fiction Australia

7 Aron op. cit.

8 www.thoughtco.com/left-brain-right-brain-1857174

9 News in English. "Norway to start a try a more flexible school start" by Nina Bergland. www.newsinenglish.no Accessed Jan 2020

10 News in English. "Norway to start a try a more flexible school start" by Nina Bergland. www.newsinenglish.no Accessed Jan 2020

11 Aron op. cit.

12 ibid.

13 ibid.

14 Carroll, L. & Tobler, J. (eds), *The Indigo Children.* (1999), Hay House USA

15 Kath McClosky, K. "Things to remember when raising indigo children", *The Indigo Children.* (1999), Carroll, L. & Tobler, J., (eds), Hay House USA.

16 Carroll, L. & Tobler, J. (eds), *The Indigo Children.* (1999), Hay House USA

17 US National Foundation for Gifted and Creative Children. *The Indigo Children.* (1999), Carroll, L. & Tobler, J., (eds), Hay House USA.

18 Feinstein, S., *Secrets Of the Teenage Brain.* (2014), SAGE, USA

19 ibid.

20 Daily Mail, Australia. "The dying light exploring the strange phenomenon of lights seen at the time of death." (May, 2020) www.dailymail.com, accessed 8 Feb 2021

21 Aron

22 Aron op. cit.

23 ibid.

24 Boyce, T., MD *The Orchid and the Dandelion*. (2019), Bluebird UK

25 Milner, J., *Raising a Screen Smart Kid*. (2019), Penguin Random House LLC USA

26 In RCH news "Celebrating achievements in allergy services"31/5.2007At

27 Smith M., Dr & Williams, S., *Gene Genius*. (2015), Harlequin Non-fiction Australia

28 www.rch.org.au

29 Aron's online checklist. hsperson.com/test/highly-sensitive-child-test/

ONE
HEART

www.ingramcontent.com/pod-product-compliance
Lightning Source LLC
Chambersburg PA
CBHW021838020426
42334CB00014B/682